ROADSIDE ATTRACTIONS

A POETIC GUIDE TO AMERICAN ODDITIES

JOHN WOJTOWICZ

To Donna,
Hope to see
you down
the road!
-John

ROADSIDE ATTRACTIONS

 Some parts of this work have appeared in slightly different form in sundry periodicals and books prior to the publication of this volume. Grateful nods to the following journals in which some of these poems or earlier versions of them first appeared:

Kansas City Voices: Biggest Balls of Twine
Coastal Shelf: Four Corners
Dead Mule School of Southern Literature: Cadillac Ranch
West Trade Review: Garden of 1000 Buddhas
Sutterville Review: Grandfather Cuts Loose the Ponies
FeezeRay: Fremont Troll, Statues of Paul Bunyan
Northern Virginia Review: Lucy the Elephant
Plainsongs: World's Largest Prairie Dog

For information about the photography used in this volume, please see the section ABOUT THE IMAGES USED IN THIS BOOK towards the end of the book. It explains wherethe images came from and their usage rights. The author and the publisher are grateful for the artists[permission to use these images in this book.

ISBN: 978-1-954895-08-9

A Parnilis Media Production – P.O. Box 1461, Media PA 19063

FOR JESS

who showed me roots nourish more than wings

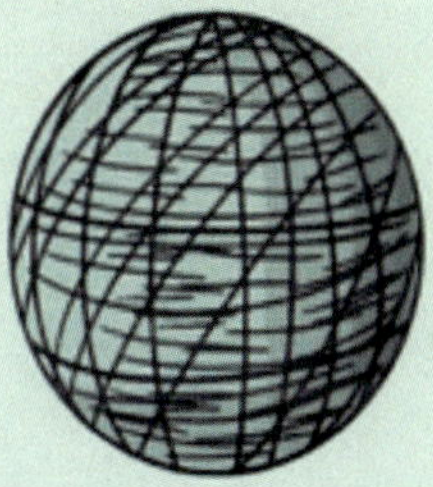

CONTENTS

Never go to Europe for a cathedral.

– Stephen Dunn

COWTOWN
RODEO

NEAR-SIGHTED

Polaris sways across night sky,
proof of planetary curves.
I drive my girl out to the rodeo,
high-waisted shorts and cowgirl boots.

We split a cigarette between us
as she manifests a Labrador and white picket fence.
I turn left at the 22ft pistol-packing
fiberglass cowboy with brick-crown Stetson.

Steer wrangling, saddle bronc, bull riding
and barrel racing. Drinking PBR
from an '84 Coleman. Kissing through halftime:
capuchin monkey riding a pony.

Later, we lay in the S-10's extended bed,
warm and wet, our greenhouse effect.
Ursa Minor bares all seven silvertip
stars at eleven and again at midnight.

What more could there be to this life?

CADILLAC RANCH

A trio of spring-breakers unload
from a '91 Chevy Starcraft,
stretching from a long ride
on the Mother Road to this cow pasture
just west of Amarillo.

In the distance, ten junk Cadillacs
gutted like exuviae
are half-buried, front ends down
facing west, single file
tail fins turned up toward the Texas sky.

Club Coupe to Sedan Deville,
day-glow dominoes.
Each lodged in sunbaked earth
at the same angle
as The Great Pyramid of Giza.

The boys pass through a makeshift
graffitied gate. Birkenstocks
atop cracked dirt. One tags
a pot leaf on the hood of an Eldorado,
another enflames the tailfins.

The last John Hancock's the driver
side, briefly satisfies, this human urge
to mark universal canvas,
leave a glossy fingerprint
among layers of fleeting hieroglyphs.

BIGGEST BALLS OF TWINE

While the progressives in Cawker City, Kansas,
promote their now oval behemoth
as a collaborative, on-going effort,
the conservatives in Darwin, Minnesota, boast
that their ball is the perfectly symmetrical
accomplishment of one man.

Both balls were started by farmers
collecting twine scraps off barn floors,
their mid-western version of Zen gardening,
wrapping rather than raking for over twenty-years.

Darwinians keep their ball enclosed
in a glass-paneled gazebo with gift shop
in contrast to the open-air pavilion in Cawker
where locals will provide twine
to anyone willing to contribute their time.

The village versus the great man,
a classic contention in the hierarchy
of accomplishments. Rival residents
have individual and communal justifications.

But they all shake their heads
when anybody mentions the enormous ball
made by a machine designed by a man in Texas
who sold his synthetic creation
to the Florida location of Ripley's Believe It
Or Not. Technically, it's made of string.

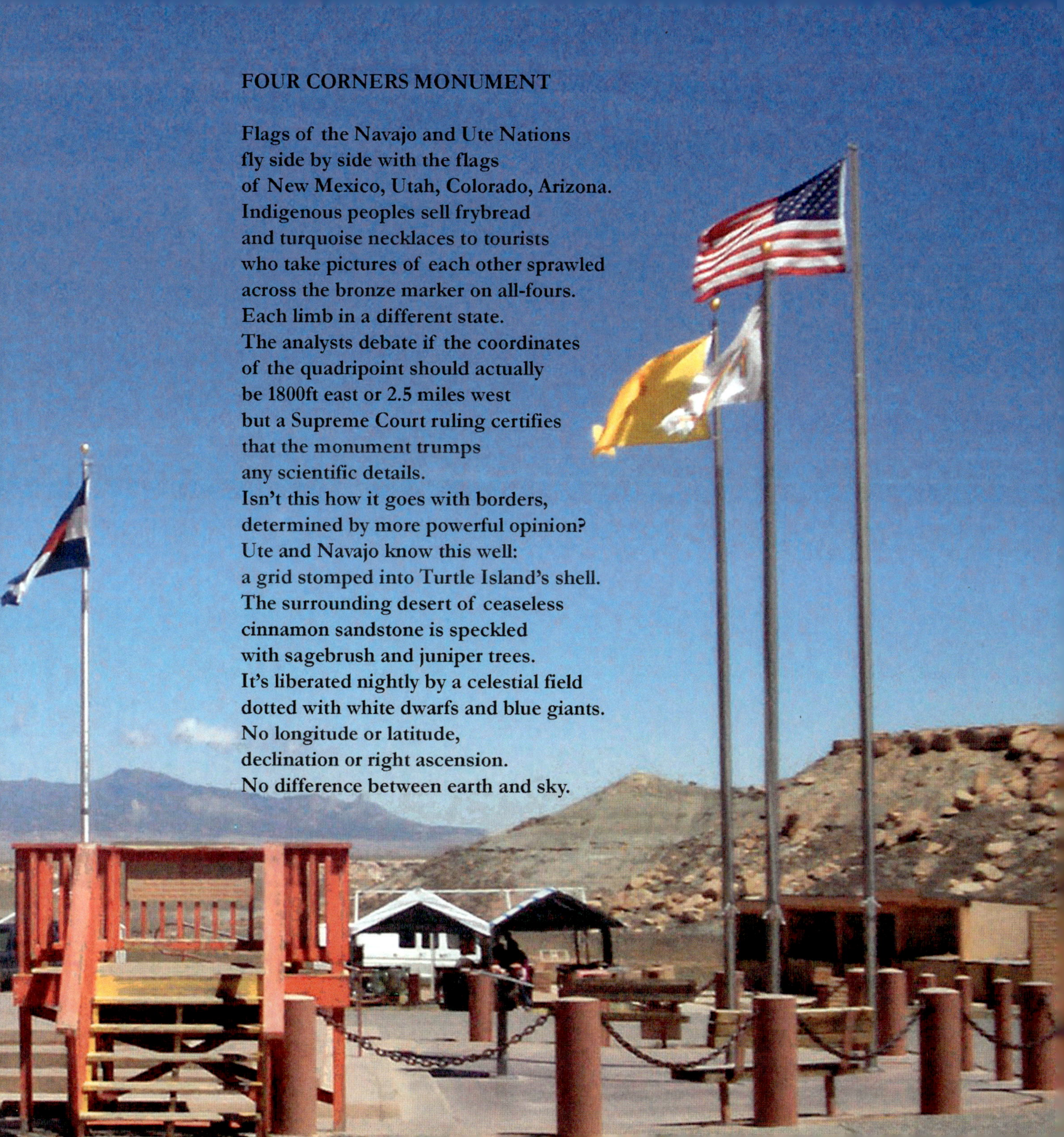

FOUR CORNERS MONUMENT

Flags of the Navajo and Ute Nations
fly side by side with the flags
of New Mexico, Utah, Colorado, Arizona.
Indigenous peoples sell frybread
and turquoise necklaces to tourists
who take pictures of each other sprawled
across the bronze marker on all-fours.
Each limb in a different state.
The analysts debate if the coordinates
of the quadripoint should actually
be 1800ft east or 2.5 miles west
but a Supreme Court ruling certifies
that the monument trumps
any scientific details.
Isn't this how it goes with borders,
determined by more powerful opinion?
Ute and Navajo know this well:
a grid stomped into Turtle Island's shell.
The surrounding desert of ceaseless
cinnamon sandstone is speckled
with sagebrush and juniper trees.
It's liberated nightly by a celestial field
dotted with white dwarfs and blue giants.
No longitude or latitude,
declination or right ascension.
No difference between earth and sky.

WORLD'S LARGEST PRAIRIE DOG

The twelve-foot pink and ochre likeness
sends drivers skirting off Exit 131
for Cactus Flat, South Dakota,
where potato-sized denizens
of a black-tailed prairie dog town
pop like Whac-a-Moles from burrow mounds.

Ninety-eight percent of the North American
population met the buffalo's fate
when settlers claimed the plains
but here pups are playful,
gossiping above ground.

Prairie dog linguists can distinguish
different high-pitched yipping calls
for *tall human in a yellow shirt*
and *short human in a green shirt*.
Human with a gun and without.

In the statue's vicinity, their burrows
are protected. Exquisite networks
of tunnels and chambers: bedrooms, bathrooms,
and nurseries. Prepared visitors
pull baby carrots from coolers.
Peanuts can be purchased for fifty cents.

What must the black-tails
make of this concrete patron saint?
Do salt-and-pepper elders tell
how under The Great One's spell
humans present gifts
in repentance for the killing contests?

Tourists aim cameras and shoot
as prairie dogs jump-yip at the sight
of *medium humans in white*
after Labor Day. It's easy to love
those who eat from the palms of your hands.

...prairie dogs have alarm calls containing descriptive information about the general size, order, and speed of approaching predators.

--Dr. Con Slobodchikoff
Biology professor and prairie dog linguist, North Arizona University

UFO WELCOME CENTER: *TILT RIGHT BOWMAN*

reads a billboard off I-26. Two silver saucers assembled
from scrap metal, stacked up like a snowman,
await behind a scruffy gas station.
SPACE PEOPLE ONLY spray painted on the fence.

The yard is a time capsule of the 20th century:
mossy cinderblocks, assorted kitchen
appliances, extension cords, empty jugs of antifreeze,
plastic lawn chairs, car batteries.

Beyond these relics, an entrance hatch reveals
a narrow hallway with a guest book
asking your name, what planet you're from.

Most visitors jot down the date, their country
or state, Planet Earth. A few wise guys
have written Mars or Jupiter, a couple wiser still
have scribbled URANUS in bold letters.

If we're being honest, this may be the epitome
of human comedy. A joke so universal
we have to be discouraged from enjoying it.
Someone always there to remind us:
Actually, it rains diamonds on Ur-a-nus.

The spacecraft's innards are constructed from
haphazard plywood, exposed wires intertwined
to power strings of Christmas lights,
an air conditioner, toilet, and cable television.

In the control room, a ladder invites passengers
up to the smaller saucer,
no connecting bolts for ease of abduction.

During the Great American Solar Eclipse,
the residents of Bowman, even those who consider
the scrapheap an eyesore, gathered around
to witness the celestial phenomenon:

cardboard eclipse glasses, cease-fire in debates
of whose moons are whose, who's a planet
and who's not. Otherworldly forces
conspiring to flicker the lights, remind us
like an interstellar vessel in the night,
of our pale-blue-dot-ness.

UFO WELCOME CENTER
BOWMAN
PLANET EARTH
UFO

NUCLEAR WASTE ADVENTURE TRAIL

"a window to the past…" – Missouri Division of Tourism

The half-mile gravel path leading up
the 75-foot disposal cell
seems less apocalyptic if trekkers avoid
brooding over the 41 acres
of radioactive rubble beneath them.

A panoramic view, spanning five rural
Missouri counties, awaits visitors at the top.

Between wars, an explosives factory
turned uranium refinery
was abandoned, barrels of sludge
left oozing into earth.

Events for astronomers and bird watchers
are scheduled monthly.

The former radiation check point
is now an interactive
interpretive center displaying
vintage Geiger counters and gas masks.

Class trips should be booked at least
a month in advance.

The EPA designed the trapezoidal sepulcher
to inter contaminate for 1000 years
in a high-tech garbage bag
concealed by layers of clay, sand, and stone.

Visitors are encouraged to Leave no Trace.
Pack in, Pack out. Give a Hoot Don't Pollute.

Locals suspect runoff culpable
for miscarriages and cancer clusters.
At the summit, high schoolers,
dubbed "glow worms," are frequently caught kissing,
distant prairie in radiant bloom.

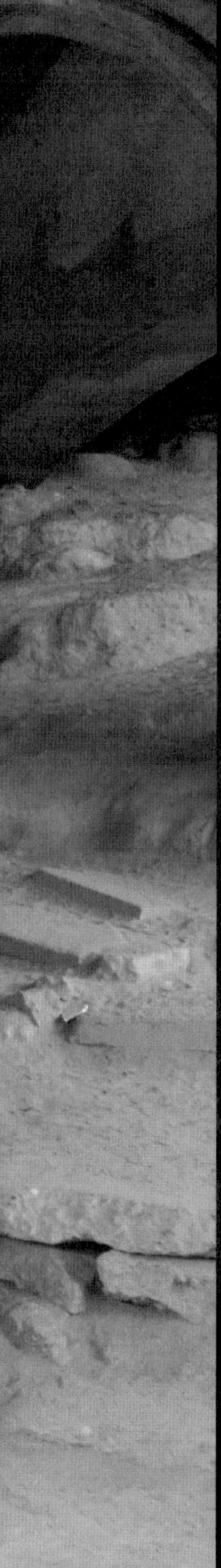

FREMONT TROLL

Under a bridge at the dead end
of a Seattle street, a shaggy eighteen-foot troll,
hubcap for an eye, glares southward.

His gangly fingers clutch
a Volkswagen Beetle with California plates
swiped from the freeway above.

After a tollbooth eliminated his occupation,
he finds outsiders and *progress*
unpalatable. Many of his neighbors share this sentiment

Artists and bartenders in studio
apartments strain to exist. Eurasian blue tits
make nests in exhaust pipes.

Before the troll took up residence,
degenerates shot dope and dumped trash
under the grimy underpass.

He curated space for himself
in a city running out of real estate, infused life
into a previously forsaken enclave.

And developers can smell a resurgence,
encroaching with peak lapels, floral ties,
wingtip oxfords: *Now we're coming to gobble you up.*

FOUNTAINS OF YOUTH

In St. Augustine, some residents
believe, Ponce De Leon
was searching for the Fountain of Youth
when he planted Spain's flag
on Florida's east coast.

Diamond Lil, former medical doctor
and Yukon gold-rush success,
claimed she discovered the Spaniard's spring
and safeguarded it within a coquina shack.
A taste of the sulfur-scented
water is still included with admission.

It's possible to circumnavigate the globe
in three months. Summit Everest
in two. Voyage to the moon
and back in under a week.
What could an explorer wish to achieve
that can't be realized in a lifetime?

In Lewes, Delaware, a few exits
past the 46-foot red-eyed golem
erupting from Dover International Speedway,
a hand-painted sign claims
that a miniature gazebo with birchbark roof
once housed the fabled fountain.

Water no longer flows but Daughters
of the American Revolution
weedwack and tell tales
of parched Queen Anne railroad men
who aimlessly traverse the Earth
covered in everlasting grease and grime.

St. Augustinians also whisper
about a centenarian society of immortal keepers.
Members meeting up for margaritas.
Ponce & Lil at the Sloppy Pelican,
shooting dice, eternally rolling doubles.

FOUNTAIN OF YOUTH

STATUES OF PAUL BUNYAN

As a newborn, Paul Bunyan was so big
it took five storks to deliver him.

In Bangor, Maine, his birth certificate
is on display at City Hall and a 31ft fiberglass likeness,
clad in buffalo plaid, towers downtown.

In anticipation of a Willie Nelson concert,
the statue sported a bedspread-sized red bandana.

The first time Paul Bunyan clapped
he shattered every window in his parent's cabin.

In a Stephen King novel, the effigy was possessed,
double-bit axe and peavey, by an ancient evil.

When Paul had a nightmare, he tossed
and turned so much he caused an earthquake.

Hometowns resist being outgrown, scorn those
who make waves. Efforts to tame
wildness often will a desire to tame other wild things.

Like some Johnny Appleseed antichrist:
Paul Bunyan felled pine trees an acre at a time.

Restlessness can disguise itself as initiative,
gluttony as success: names emblazoned
on skyscrapers like faces on the wall of a steakhouse.

Bunyan's pipe was so large it had to be packed with a shovel.

Minnesota is littered with graven images,
towns claiming birthright,
each attempting to cultivate his lore in local soil.

Ackley displays Paul's oversized crib
alongside a two-story rendering:
mill belts for suspenders, beard of resin-soaked twine.

Bemidji lays claim to his coffee mug, yo-yo,
moccasins, toothbrush, dice, and toenail clippings.

Paul Bunyan and Babe's footprints formed The Great Lakes.

A 1-ton walleye hooked by the hulking woodsman
is beached near a Burger King in Rush City.
His 110-ton granite anchor is docked in Ortonville.

On the shores of Birch Lake, there's a 17ft fiberglass
likeness of his buxom dark-haired sweetheart.

*After Lucette's Ojibwe mother and English father
died of smallpox, she was raised by a sleuth of bears.*

Bemidji, Minn.
PAUL
BUNYAN
1937

Her bouffant-style dress exposes biceps
capable of fixing a cracked wagon wheel with one hand
while frying grit cakes with the other.

Paul Bunyan perpetually cleared land from the Atlantic to the Pacific.

Even soulmates need to replenish their tinder,
sit together around a connubial fire.

In Portland, a statue towers across the street
from the Dancing Bare Gentleman's Club.
Loneliness is a flame that collects its own kindling.

Paul fashioned Mt. Hood by piling rocks on top of his campfire.

An aging Bunyan in Klamath greets visitors
at *The Trees of Mystery*, booming voice
originating from the gift shop, Wizard of Oz style.

In his prime, Paul Bunyan could cleave a redwood with one swing.

If by evading roots, a man could avoid
being felled, Paul might've leveled North America.

When his arms finally gave out,
he trailed his axe, forming The Grand Canyon.

Nature is both the turtle and the hare.
Paul Bunyan's grave is in Kelliher. Shaded by a hearty pine.

GRANDFATHER CUTS LOOSE THE PONIES

One of the most-seen public artworks in Washington State
is only half finished. There wasn't enough money to sculpt the basket. – Seattle Times

The hubbub of hooves was replaced by the hum
of industrial tillers, giving way to wheat fields
and fruit ranches, cattle ranges sensitive to overgrazing.

In early spring, buckaroos corralled the remaining mustangs
at the mouth of Crab Creek, herds laden
with newborn colts and pregnant mares.

The Last Grand Roundup— the final act of the Old West.

Fifteen steel horses, now oxidized to a rich vermillion,
gallop towards the crest of a rocky bluff
overlooking the Columbia River.

Dreamcatcher sunsets cast the long shadows
motorists see from the Wanapum Vista Viewpoint.

Native tribes, also confined to reservations, tell an origin story
depicting the Great Spirit pouring
all the variations of life from a vast basket,
entrusting man to revere the balance.

Are we content to merely mourn the casualties
of our greed, ceaseless loggers
erecting monuments to commemorate clear-cut trees?

IGLOO

IGLOO CITY

The proprietor envisioned his remote motel
as an arctic Wigwam Village
with guests quartered in an 80ft snow hut
instead of concrete teepees.

Nowadays, travelers pull over to take a leak,
peak at the crumbling infrastructure.
One man's pit stop is another's unfulfilled dream.

Snow conceals weather-beaten urethane
and crude graffiti. Fifty-eight dormer
windows frame rugged Alaskan mountain-views
from the inside of unrealized rooms.

Halfway between Anchorage and Fairbanks
it's easy to imagine warm lights
projecting from each boarded-up opening,
coarse laughter from the bar.

Would-be lodgers, bellies full of black coffee,
heading off to Wonder Lake.
Reeling-in postcards of the 42ft Santa Claus
in North Pole. Denali cascading
through their fishing nets.

Despite zoning men equipped with red pens,
he was steadfast in the belief
that his happiness depended on more sheetrock
for a personal penthouse suite.

Even from the top floor, he couldn't see the snow
for the flakes. Cycles of chilling
and thawing solidify an igloo.

When occupied, temperatures can reach
a balmy 60° even when it's -50°, body heat
moonlighting as a furnace. Like dreams,
igloos dissipate if permanently inhabited.

BIG DUCK

"Duck architecture" refers to buildings designed
in the shape of what they hawk:

coffee pot coffee shops, banana split
ice cream parlors, hot dog stands
topped with relish and mustard. Shoe stores…

Enthusiasts can check out a bookshelf
shaped library in Kansas City
or an Apple Store modeled
after a Macbook Pro in Chicago.

The forerunner was a 30ft peking duck
that housed a store selling peking ducks.

The Big Duck has since been repurposed
as a Long Island tourist center
peddling regional maps and history books.

Most things, over time, start to retail
more than their pragmatic selves.

In Ohio, a seven-story Longaberger
basket that once held the Longaberger Headquarters
is slated to become a high-end hotel
where guests can curl up like kittens.

There's a certain reverence, on this urn-shaped
planet which now markets
refined existence, reserved for holes
poked in the container:

escaped zoo animals, art on the lam
from museums, architecture
that's waddled out of nursery rhymes.

Around Christmas, locals gather to swath
the waterfowl in lights and garland.
Kids sing "duck carols" to lionize
more than the sum of ferrocement feathers.

No one is going to drive out of the way for normal
– Gary Greff, scrap metal artist

ENCHANTED HIGHWAY

There's a bouquet of ring-neck pheasants
who could gobble up tourists like ticks
and a grasshopper as tall as a saguaro cactus

who feasts on giant stalks of golden wheat.
Pterodactyl sized geese
orbit the ten-story ellipse of an eye

and silhouettes of deer who could trample
a Winnebago haunt the shoulder.
Fish with spots like juggling rings leap

from a lake suspended in mid-air
while 40-foot tin men eagerly usher
spellbound travelers into the town of Regent.

If drivers weren't seduced off Exit 72
and enticed for 30 miles across perpetual prairie
even the town's ghosts might pack
celestial suitcases and head down the freeway.

A prodigious profile of Teddy Roosevelt
waving atop a 50ft stallion
presides over the town's boisterous revival.

Regent's high school, pupil-less for years,
has metamorphosed into a medieval motel
with on-site tavern. A king-size knight
and copper-breathing dragon scrap out back.

Sightseers who sleepover are welcome
to unwind in an eight-person Jacuzzi
effervescing in the former principal's office.

Inside a storage shed, a 70-foot spider-web
awaits to ensnare travelers but old-school
farmers refuse to lease their land. Some residents
would rather fade away than transfigure.

CABAZON DINOSAURS & OTHER STORIES

Along the I-10 freeway heading towards Palm Springs,
Mr. Rex, a 65ft tall T- rex, and Dinny,
a 150ft long brontosaurus, were constructed as some sort
of shotcrete-mâché tribute to the glory days.

Dinny's current higher power willed a Creationist Museum
in his belly with exhibits explaining how God
created dinosaurs and Adam
in the same six-day stretch about 6,000 years ago.

Between Cincinnati and Lexington,
off I-75, there's a scale-model of The Great Ark
built according to biblical dimensions: 510 feet long, 85 feet wide,
and 51 feet high. Complete with animatronic
Noah and life-like velociraptors.

The curators of these attractions claim that giant reptiles,
like all creatures, were vegetarian
back in the days of Eden. Before the whole Eve incident
unleashed bloodshed and death on Earth.

Good science is open to inquisition, good faith
is unquestioning. Dinosaurs didn't bode well
in the post-flood world and, like so many other fauna,
have since gone extinct: habitat loss,
overpopulation, the rise of an invasive species.

The commissioner of the seven-story Christ of the Ozarks
hired a renowned dinosaur sculptor
to construct his Jurassic Messiah. Upon the statue's unveiling,
he decreed it more beautiful than Michelangelo's *Jesus.*
Locals have decreed it:
The Statue of Willie Nelson Wearing a Dress.

Perspectives have their perks. The gospel of the dinosaurs
gives authority to dragons and sea serpents,
demonstrates the ability of man to endure beyond possibility
but limits the opportunity for on-going evolution.

Tourists can climb up to look out from between Mr. Rex's
serrated teeth. From this vantage point,
it's easy to empathize with Dinny,
gravid with his own truth– Mr. Rex a goliath byproduct
of original sin, bearing down upon him.

MAMMY'S CUPBOARD

Fried chicken, collard greens, and bake beans
are served (after tours of antebellum mansions
made famous by *Gone with the Wind*)
inside the hoop-skirt of a 28-foot, red-brick,
bandanna-wearing, southern mammy.

Tuesday through Saturday, waitresses
stack plates, clank silverware,
and slice famous banana caramel pies,
under cypress support beams
salvaged from a bulldozed cotton gin house.

In the 60's, management softened
the red of her cheeks, unhooked her horseshoe earrings,
ceased running ads that proclaimed:
Mammy's vittles will nurse chil-uns
now aged into good ol' boys and gals.

Recent owners restored her crumbling arms
and serving tray, refurbished the arched
windows of her housedress, claiming the blueprints
more O'Hara-esque. Frommer's advises
checking all political correctness at the door.

They've lightened her complexion, rebranded
as kitsch— *a throwback to the Golden Age of Hollywood.*
But nothing revises half-empty breasts, the cries
of empty-bellied infants. A young master
asleep in his crib, milk dribbling from his satiated mouth.

Sorry WE'RE
CLOSED

LUCY THE ELEPHANT

She was built for luring the wealthy
to her open-air howdah
where parcels of Jersey shoreline
could be selected for purchase.

Hand-fashioned beams within
support her six story exterior
of hammered tin. A spiral staircase entrance
is tucked in her left hind leg.

Twenty windows and two eyes
survey what was once
sand dunes and scrub pines,
spume the color of ivory.

Nondescript condominiums
surround her now, buildings
with the privilege of beauty
without having to be beautiful.

Ears like swimming pools, trunk
like a water slide, tourists take photos
and guided tours. Friends
provide festive pedicures.

Her ashen paint records hurricanes
and tropical storms. Lightning
has struck twice but still she towers
with a lumbering majesty.

The desire for the remarkable
is not as great as the demand
for the ordinary; zoomorphic
architecture never really took off.

But who says the novel can't be practical?
Lucy's been a tavern, restaurant,
real-estate office, the summer home
of a doctor and his family.

A rarely vacant thirty-foot
beagle-shaped bed and breakfast
in Idaho embodies the concept:
bedroom in the belly,
bathroom in the rear.

LADY'S LEG SUNDIAL

The founder of the of Sun Aura Nudist Resort
argued in a Northern Indiana court that the constitution
doesn't decree citizens must wear clothes:
My Country 'Tis of Thee, Sweet Land of Liberty.

The subsequent owner erected a 63ft high-kicking lady's leg
properly angled to cast punctual shade
upon a red, white, and blue pedestal.
Convenient for the wristwatchless naturalist.

Spectators are welcome to gawk at the plexiglass
and plywood Rockette-style sundial.
The rest of the 300 forested acers
(including the heart-shaped lake) are Members Only.

There's something exact about submerging
in the element of the world, embracing your whole
body as both instrument and ornament,
playing cribbage and pickleball without constraint.

Around Saint Patty's, Sun Aura officially kicks
their season off with an Erin-Go-Braless mixer.
In preparation, colonists repaint the sundial's slender gam
fully exposed to the warmth of mid-day sun.

JOLLY GREEN GIANT

Orphaned by his parent company
but beloved by his adopted town – Minnesota Daily

On the final day of Blue Earth's *Giant Days* festival,
children follow size 78 lima-bean-green
footprints downtown for a mid-summer parade.

The 55ft gardener, resplendent in his verdant tunic,
models, as always, atop his 8ft base with staircase.
Summer vacationers pose for pictures between his legs.

We wish for children to believe in the delicate magic
that rarely breeches our own somber flowerbeds,
having traded the security of frayed blankets
for the predictability of reason and logic.

Vehicles heading to Yellowstone and the Black Hills
are coaxed from strict velocities, yielding
to back-seat appeals and driver curiosities.

Children are our best excuse to make bad time,
bow to the unbeatable clock—a logical reason
to pull off the highway in pursuit
of a fiberglass goliath, grinning above the tree line.

On Giant's Eve, parents stay up late with quarts
of weatherproof paint, custodians of wonder,
sowers of seeds, again and again, heartened by the sprouts.

Welcome to
Blue Earth

BLUE WHALE OF CATOOSA

A few years past pearl and a year short of coral;
there's no traditional gift
for a 34th wedding anniversary.

One retired zookeeper crafted an 80-foot-long blue whale
from concrete and pipe for his wife
who collected miniature whale figurines.

Old Blue still swims in a little pond off Route 66:
slide spouting from his side,
diving platform perched on his raised tail,
jaunty little baseball cap.

Whales are the grand pooh-bahs
of planet earth. Tongues as heavy as elephants,
blood vessels so wide
you could backstroke through them.

Old Blue's massive open-mouth smile
welcomes visitors inside. Children's laughter echoes
from all eighteen porthole windows.

Whales' resonances can rival jet engines
and have continued to amplify as grunts of maritime
traffic and groans of glacial melting
block calls from reaching would-be lovers.

Divers report feeling these songs
more than hearing them. And isn't that the sure sign
of a successful gesture of love?

Not a thing smuggled from the bottom
of the sea but a bellow loud enough to attract attention
across the ocean, the Mother Road.

Still, whales don't mate for life
or even for gestation, and no matter how grand,
a one-night stand won't satisfy
voracious human standards for true love.

Daily intimacies sustain us, gobbled up like six tons
of krill. 34 years of morning coffee,
knowing just how much creamer. No need for words.

GARDEN OF ONE THOUSAND BUDDHAS

In the middle of rural western Montana,
a Rinpoche noticed the land
looked like a lotus flower and asked his disciple,
an heir to the Hyatt Hotel fortune,
to pull off Highway 93 onto White Coyote Road.

He remembered the location from a vision
and cultivated a garden in the form
of an eight-spoked dharmachakra. At the center
a sculpture of the Great Wisdom Mother,
her base crafted using melted-down
firearms, an effigy to peace on earth.

Yum Chenmo sits, radiant in red, blue, yellow,
and gold, surrounded by semi-circle walls
adorned with chalk-white statues:
1000 mini-stupas from India form the outer wheel.
1000 Montana-made buddhas adorn the spokes.

By the pond, a rancher smokes a Marlboro
among eight large buddhas in different stages
of enlightenment, prayer flags waving in prairie wind.
The mountains still wear thick snowcaps;
he's stopped here to rest, tired from clinging to worries
of when the snow will melt in the valley.

For one cigarette, he is but another buddha
Ushnisha overtaking his Stetson.
There's a lot of Zen in ranching but at its core
caring for animals or people
consists mostly of preparing for tomorrow.

Each night the buddhas awake
without opening their eyes, utter a collective om
that resonates from the cobalt Mission Mountains.
In his bed, the rancher notices his breath,
doesn't reach for the unlit cigarette
resting on his nicotine-stained nightstand.

FLOORING
856-455-1126
CARPET • VINY
HARDWOOD • T
RESIDENTIAL-COMMER

FAR-SIGHTED

Clad in a sleeveless rouge tunic,
a sun-faded sixteen-foot fiberglass
Norseman stands guard
outside Orr's Carpet and Flooring
off NJ Route 77.

I drive past this muscular giant
almost daily, without pausing
for a quick photo or closer look.

Have I lost an eye for local wonders?
I suppose even the Apostolic Palace
eventually just becomes the pope's house.

On vacation, I might find myself
skirting off an unknown exit
for a glimpse. Paying an admission fee.
Buying a miniature Viking statue
and six-dollar corn dog.

But here, he's part of the scenery–
another timeworn tree with horned helmet
and gunslinger mustache;
a landmark where you could tell
an out-of-town friend to take a left.

This morning, light snow creates
an iridescent cape, concealing peeling paint,
a sort of corrective lens
that brings him into focus again.

ABOUT THE IMAGES USED IN THIS BOOK

The images used to illustrate these poems were collected from many different sources, some copyrighted and used by express permission of the artist, some released into the public domain or under Creative Commons licenses, and used without the endorsement of the artist. Every effort has been made to credit and respect the creators of the visual art in this volume. Please contact the publisher for further information or to correct any errors we may have made in attribution.

DOODLES ON OPENING PAGES

Line drawings by Mikaela Simon of Doodle All Day, based at https://www.etsy.com/shop/doodlealldayy

NEAR-SIGHTED

Postcard image courtesy Kimberly Paynter kpaynter@whyy.org Logo courtesy of Cowtown Rodeo, Pilesgrove, New Jersey.

CADILLAC RANCH

Cadillac Ranch built west of Amarillo off Route 66 by Stanley Marsh in 1974. Photograph by Richie Diestterheft released under a Creative Commons license, cropped to fit the page

BIGGEST BALLS OF TWINE

Twine background texture in the public domain. Sketchbook drawings copyrighted and used by kind permission of Chandler O'Leary (chanderloleary.com), author of The Best Coast, A Road Trip Atlas (Sasquatch Books, 2020).

FOUR CORNERS MONUMENT

Photograph by David Jolley, 2007, released under a Creative Commons Attribution 3.0 unported license.

WORLD'S LARGEST PRAIRIE DOG

Historic souvenir postcard from the 1960s, believed to be in the public domain.

NUCLEAR WASTE ADVENTURE TRAIL

Image in the public domain, edited by Matt Lake.

FREMONT TROLL

Photograph by David Herrera, released under a Creative Commons 2.0 share-alike license.

FOUNTAINS OF YOUTH

Background photography by Matt Lake, 2021. Postcards courtesy of the Boston Public Library, released under a Creative Commons share-alike 2.0 license

STATUES OF PAUL BUNYAN

Postcards from Matt Lake's collection, in the public domain.

GRANDFATHER CUTS LOOSE THE PONIES

Photograph by J (Antarctica5000), released under a Creative Commons share-alike 3.0 license.

IGLOO CITY

Photograph by Diego Delso, (http://delso.photo) released under a Creative Commons share-alike license.

BIG DUCK

Photograph by Mike Peel (www.mikepeel.net), released under a Creative Commons share-alike 4.0 license. Cropped and edited by Matt Lake, 2021

ENCHANTED HIGHWAY

Photograph of scrap metal artwork Grasshoppers in the Field by Skvader (1999), released under a Creative Commons share-alike license 4.0.

MAMMY'S CUPBOARD

Photograph from the Carol M. Highsmith Archive collection at the Library of Congress, released into the public domain by the photographer.

CABAZON DINOSAURS & OTHER STORIES

Photograph by Jllm06 (2009) released under a Creative Commons Z 1.0 Universal Public Domain license

LADY'S LEG SUNDIAL

Photograph Mandy Crandell (planetgloom.etsy.com, www.instagram.com/planetgloom)

LUCY THE ELEPHANT

Photograph by Acroterion, released under a Creative Commons share-alike 4.0 license.

BLUE WHALE OF CATOOSA

Photography by Erica Chang, released under a Creative Commons 3.0 unported license.

JOLLY GREEN GIANT

Image in the public domain.

GARDEN OF ONE THOUSAND BUDDHAS

Photograph by Montanabw (2012), released under a Creative Commons 3.0 attribution and share-alike license.

FAR-SIGHTED

Image of the Viking flooring mannequin by Jessica Monahan.

I would be remiss if I did not thank the village of folks who helped in pulling these poems out of the void:

To R.G. Evans has selflessly encouraged my poetic journey over the last fifteen years

To Peter Murphy and Murphy Writing of Stockton University for propping the door wide open. Many of these poems were started or enhanced through your programs.

To Anthony Palma and Brooke Palma for their friendship and warm welcome into the Mad Poets Society

To J.C. Todd, Barb Daniels, Cat Doty, and Emari DiGorigio for helping these poems slip into something more comfortable

To Celeste Doaks and Octavia McBride-Ahebee for their guidance and support in the writing of Mammy's Cupboard

To Matt Lake for cheerleading this project and giving it public life

To my parents for their never-ending support and encouragement

To Aubrey who never leaves a question unasked and Jack who is always up for a good belly laugh

About the Author

John Wojtowicz grew up working on his family's azalea and rhododendron nursery in the backwoods of what Ginsberg dubbed "nowhere Zen New Jersey." Currently, he pays the bills as a social worker and an adjunct professor. On weekends, he enjoys grooving to folk music in the Pine Barrens. His poetry has been nominated 3x for Pushcart Prizes and has been published in numerous journals including: Tule Review, El Portel, The Mom Egg, Naugatuck River Review, Driftwood, Glassworks Magazine, Patterson Literary Review, Jelly Bucket, and Spitball: The Baseball Literary Magazine. His poems have also been featured on Rowan University's Writer's Roundtable on 89.7 WGLS-FM and in Princeton University's 2021 Unique Minds: Creative Voices exhibit at the Lewis Center for the Arts. He serves as the Local Lyrics contributor for the Mad Poet Society's Blog. Check out www.johnwojtowicz.com for updates. He lives with his wife and two children in Upper Deerfield, NJ.

Made in the USA
Middletown, DE
05 September 2023

37531084R00031